I0421581

This Belongs To:

Published by Two Rivers Publishing
TwoRiversPublishing.com

www.ingramcontent.com/pod-product-compliance
Lightning Source LLC
Chambersburg PA
CBHW060427290526
45791CB00002B/889
* 9 7 8 1 0 7 5 9 7 9 5 5 2 *